MW00954521

# The BOSTON MARATHON

Published by Creative Education, Inc.

123 South Broad Street, Mankato, MN 56001

Designed by Rita Marshall with the help of Thomas Lawton

Cover illustration by Rob Day, Lance Hidy Associates

Copyright © 1993 by Creative Education, Inc.

Photography by Allsport, David Brownell, Duomo,
Light Sources, Anthony Neste, Denise Rocco, Victah Sailer,
Stock Boston, Wide World Photos

Printed in the United States

Library of Congress Cataloging-in-Publication Data

Kulper, Eileen, 1965–

The Boston Marathon / Eileen Kulper.

Summary: Presents highlights in the history of the Boston
Marathon, an event that has been held annually since 1897.

ISBN 0-88682-536-9

1. Boston Marathon—History—Juvenile literature.
[1. Boston Marathon—History.]  1. Title.       92-4110

                                                CIP

GV1065.22.B67K85   1992                          AC

796.42'5'0974461—dc20

# The BOSTON MARATHON

EILEEN KULPER

3035800008 1496

CREATIVE EDUCATION INC.

"I hope no one will run very crazy," said Gelindo Bordin of Italy. "Sometimes they don't respect the right way to run the marathon. There's no strategy, just crazy running." Bordin, winner of the 1988 Olympic Marathon, was gearing up for 1990's Boston Marathon. "They" were the East Africans—the Kenyans, Ethiopians, and Tanzanians who had dominated the race the year before.

*Gelindo Bordin (center).*

*The Africans set a fast pace.*

Bordin would not get his wish, however. The gun signaled the start of the race and the Africans took off. The first mile of the twenty-six-mile race was clocked at 4:26. Juma Ikangaa from Tanzania was an early leader. Ikangaa had finished second the previous two years. He was determined not to take second place a third year in a row. At every mile marker for the first ten miles he set a new record. He hit ten miles at 46:53—a time that was twenty-eight seconds faster than the course record.

Gelindo Bordin trailed behind Ikangaa. Bordin knew the pace was too fast for him, and decided to run his own race. Ikangaa stretched his lead. After breaking away at 15.5 miles, he built his lead to 120 yards. At nineteen miles, however, Ikangaa was laboring. At twenty miles his leg began to cramp.

Then he hit Heartbreak Hill.

## HOW IT ALL BEGAN

The modern-day marathon has its roots in an ancient Greek legend. During the Greco-Persian Wars, King Darius of Persia set out to attack the city of Athens. Along the way, however, Darius's army was defeated at Marathon, twenty-four miles from Athens. According to the story, a man named Pheidippides ran all the way from Marathon to Athens to tell the Athenians of the unexpected victory. As soon as he had told his news, he fell to the ground and died.

*The start of the marathon.*

In the early 1890s, two Frenchmen, Pierre de Coubertin and Michel Breal, decided to revive the ancient Greek Olympic games. Breal suggested that the 1896 games include a race in honor of the Pheidippides legend. Twenty-five runners took part in that first Olympic Marathon, held in Athens. The winner was Spiridon-Louis, a Greek.

One of the runners in the 1896 Olympic Marathon was Arthur Blake. Inspired by the event, Blake returned to his home in Boston, where he and his fellow Boston Athletic Association members organized a race of their own.

*The Boston Marathon takes runners through country, town, and city.*

## THE STARTING LINE

Seven months after the first Olympic Marathon, fifteen men assembled at Metcalfe's Mill in Ashland, Massachusetts. It was Patriot's Day—the day commemorating Paul Revere's famous 1775 ride through the streets of Boston, when he warned Boston citizens, "The British are coming!" It seemed an appropriate day for a race through Boston.

Precisely at 12:15 P.M., on April 19, 1897, starter Tom Burke scraped the toe of his boot across a narrow dirt road in front of Metcalfe's Mill. "That's the starting line, gents," he said, and called the field to order. He read out the numbers and fifteen men answered. The race would finish at Irvington Street oval in downtown Boston. The course was 24.5 miles.

Despite its humble start, the first Boston Marathon turned into quite an exciting

event. Several hundred people gathered to watch the runners take off from Metcalfe's Mill. Many spectators brought their bicycles with them so they could pedal back to Boston alongside the runners. Each runner was followed by someone on a bicycle— usually a child—who carried water and maybe some oranges or lemons for energy.

*A volunteer offers an orange to a runner.*

*Medical personnel come to a racer's aid.*

The roads were unpaved and dry. The runners and cyclists stirred up so much dust that some of them had trouble breathing and fell by the wayside. The runners were also slowed by the boots and long pants they were wearing. At that time, the idea of exercising to stay in shape was unheard of. There were no lightweight sports clothes or high-tech running shoes, so the men ran in their everyday clothes. Their boots were thick-soled and weighed at least a pound. They needed to wear shoes this thick in order to run on the rutted roads.

McDermott even stopped to have his legs massaged. Somehow he finished the race, ten pounds lighter than when he'd started and not very enthusiastic about the sport. "I doubt I shall ever run in a marathon race again," he was overheard saying at the finish line. His time of 2:55:10 would not be very impressive today, especially since the race was almost two miles shorter than today's race. In those early days, however, it was impressive just to finish.

Ultimately, a man named J.J. McDermott took the lead. At the sixteen-mile mark at Newton Lower Falls, McDermott went out in front and continued to lead the rest of the race. But he paid the price, as every marathoner does. He ran into a funeral procession, causing two electric cars to stall. He stopped five times from Boston College to the finish. At one point

*Australian Rob de Castella, winner of the 1986 Boston Marathon.*

*The modern Boston race covers the standard marathon distance of 26 miles, 385 yards.*

## TARZAN BROWN

Perhaps the most talented man ever to run the Boston Marathon was Ellison M. Brown. Brown, or "Tarzan," as most people called him, was an Indian from the Narragansett Reservation in Rhode Island. He ran—and won—his first Boston Marathon in 1936, and won again in 1939. What was amazing was the way he did it. He did not train at all; instead, he won through pure strength and raw talent.

Tarzan Brown lived in poverty with his wife and four children in a tarpaper shack in a clearing in the woods. The shack had no running water and no kitchen, and there were only two small rooms for the entire family. Tarzan Brown had no coach and no equipment. He showed up to run in a shirt made from an old quilt.

When the runners lined up at the start of the Boston Marathon, no one had ever heard of Tarzan Brown. But that would soon change.

McDermott's career as a marathoner may have been brief, but the Boston Marathon was just beginning. Eventually it would become the United State's most prestigious road race.

*The amazing Ellison M. Brown.*

*New Zealand's Allison Roe, the women's champion in 1981.*

The gun went off and so did Tarzan Brown. He took off at such a blistering pace that no one even noticed him. At the six-mile marker in Framingham, he was five hundred yards ahead of the leader. No man in history has ever had such a large lead so early in the race. He had even gone out ahead of the press truck. When the reporters in the press truck reached Framingham, the timer asked, "What kept you guys?" The reporters said they were just following the leader. The timer replied, "You missed him—he went through here about two or three minutes ago." Baffled, the press truck sped up to try to catch the unknown runner who was leading the race.

*Competitors in the 1925 Boston Marathon.*

*Steve Jones of Great Britain won the 1988 New York City Ma*

*A marathon photographer goes after the perfect shot.*

Throughout the entire race Brown kept increasing his lead. By the time he reached the hills of Newton at the fifteen-mile marker, he was nine hundred yards ahead of his closest opponent—a distance equivalent to nine football fields.

*Brown crosses the finish line of the 1936 race.*

Brown continued this pace in the Newton hills. In the meantime, another runner was trying to catch up with Brown. John A. Kelley had won the race the year before and was the favorite for this year's marathon. Realizing he was not the leader, Kelley pushed himself in one of the greatest runs of his career. He sped through the town of Wellesley. After twenty miles, at Boston College, Kelley and Brown were racing evenly.

Kelley noticed Brown starting to slow. He knew the pace would get to him and decided that this was where he would make his move. At the top of Heartbreak Hill, Kelley reached over and in a friendly way, as if to say "good race," he patted Brown on the bottom.

Brown looked up and took off like a rabbit. Kelley never caught him after that. Not only did he not catch him, he lost sight of Brown for the rest of the race.

Brown had such a comfortable lead that at Coolidge Corner, two miles before the end of the race, he stopped running and began walking and jogging instead. He knew the entire time he would win the race. This was just an Olympic tryout for him. And now that he was assured of a spot on the Olympic team, Brown decided not to push himself for the last two miles.

Brown finished with a time of 2:33:40. What time would he have finished with if he had actually run the entire race? No one will ever know.

*Chairbound racers compete in the Boston Marathon.*

# K. SWITZER'S RACE

"I don't discriminate against women," said Jock Semple, the Boston Marathon organizer. "They're just not allowed to run in my race." Semple said this in the late 1960s, when the rule against women competing in the marathon was still in force. But in 1967, one woman proved that some rules are made to be broken.

*The 1981 runners pass through a brownstone neighborhood.*

Katherine Switzer was a twenty-year-old junior at Syracuse University. Her coach, Arnie Briggs, was a longtime friend of Jock Semple. But the two men disagreed on the issue of allowing women to take part in the Boston Marathon. In spite of Semple's rule, Arnie Briggs encouraged Switzer to enter the race. He spent months preparing her for the event. One day, after a thirty-mile run, he pronounced her ready to run the race and gave her the entry form to fill out. "K. Switzer" was sent an official race number.

On Wednesday, April 19, 1967, it was raining and sleeting. Katherine Switzer waited at the start, accompanied by Briggs and her boyfriend, Tom Miller. When the other runners realized there was a woman in the pack, many of them talked with her. Several even asked to have their pictures taken with her. Clearly the runners were intrigued by Switzer, and happy to see a woman join the competition.

The gun sounded and the runners were off. But this was not to be an ordinary race. A commotion arose near the four-mile marker, when the press learned that a woman was running the marathon. "Hey, it's a girl!" the reporters shouted. The press truck honked and plowed its way toward Switzer. Cameras clicked and reporters fired all kinds of questions.

*Joan Benoit won the women's race in 1979 and 1983.*

*Pages 20–21: Spectators cheer on the runners.*

Suddenly a man jumped off the truck and began yelling. He was Will Cloney, one of the guardians of the race. Cloney shouted at Briggs, demanding to know why a woman was running in the Boston Marathon—and with an official number, too! Briggs tried to tell him it was all right, that Switzer had trained to run a marathon, just like any other entrant. But Cloney continued to shout.

In the midst of all the chaos, Switzer kept running, trying to get away from all the reporters. Then she heard footsteps behind her. She felt someone pulling at her. Jock Semple was trying to pull her number off. "Get out of my race!" he screamed furiously. "You're not supposed to be in my race!"

At this point Switzer's boyfriend got mad—so mad that he hit Semple with a cross-body check that sent him tumbling. As soon as Semple hit the ground, Miller, Switzer, and Briggs took off into the crowd of runners.

*Despite Jock Semple's attempt to interfere, Katherine Switzer finished the 1967 race.*

This incident marked the end of the friendship between Jock Semple and Arnie Briggs. It would be ten years before they spoke again.

Switzer and her two companions ran the rest of the race undisturbed. Switzer felt tired, but determined. She knew she had to finish the race, even if it was on her hands and knees. She didn't want to give the skeptics a chance to gloat.

The trio crossed the finish line with a time of 4:20:00. Switzer had made history.

*Timekeepers are positioned throughout the course.*

She was the first woman to run the Boston Marathon with an official number. The reporters, having waited in the rain and cold for Switzer to finish the race, asked her if she competed in the marathon to further women's rights. "I just wanted to run," she replied.

Katherine Switzer's historic race helped pave the way for other women runners. Five years later, in 1972, women were granted official status in the Boston Marathon.

*The East Africans dominated the 1988 race.*

## AFRICANS DOMINATE

In 1988, Africa was the only continent that had not produced a Boston Marathon winner. But this would be the Africans' year. They had a large and impressive delegation: Kenya sent fifteen of its best runners, including Ibrahim Hussein, who had won the New York City Marathon in 1987, and the Tanzanian group was led by Juma Ikangaa, who in 1986 had been ranked the world's number-one marathoner. In fact, until the Ethiopians pulled out of the race, it looked as though the Africans would fill the top twenty spots. And all it would take was one African in the top spot to make Boston Marathon history.

*Ibrahim Hussein was the 1988 winner, with Juma Ikangaa a close second.*

The Africans faced plenty of competition, however. Several countries, including Finland and Great Britain, were using the Boston Marathon as an Olympic trial. They sent only their best runners, the fastest of whom would go on to compete in the Olympics. The marathon field also included two-time Boston Marathon champ Geoff Smith and former world-record holder Steve Jones. Besides Hussein, two other previous New York City Marathon winners, Orlando Pizzolato and Gianni Poli, were also running.

*Wet roads don't slow the runners down.*

*The marathon course winds through the Boston suburb of Brookline.*

*Orlando Pizzolato, two-time winner of the New York City Marathon.*

At exactly twelve o'clock noon the gun went off. The runners took advantage of the forty-eight-degree temperature; they clocked the first mile (all downhill) at 4:31. After the first three miles, a pack of three dozen competitors took the lead.

Steve Jones, Juma Ikangaa, and Geoff Smith stayed with the pack. So did number twenty-three, Ibrahim Hussein. Hussein was known to be a steady competitor, but not fast. He was running his fifth marathon in a year. Two months earlier, he had placed second in the Tokyo Marathon. Now he wanted to prove to himself that he could run two marathons within a short time span, and still finish with a good time.

The leaders continued to race as a pack, running abreast of each other. On the outskirts of Framingham, twenty-six runners passed the five-mile mark at 23:42. The pack was still holding tight. The pace was blistering and no one thought it would continue throughout the race.

The runners hit Natick, the ten-mile mark, at 47:57. At this point several runners had to back off because the pace was too fast. Ikangaa, Hussein, Smith, and Jones all continued to keep up, however.

With Hussein and Ikangaa leading the pack, the runners reached the halfway point. At 1:03:10, the pace was quick. But fast splits in the Boston Marathon mean nothing. The Newton hills still lay ahead —and, as expected, the hills took their toll. The field splintered and the pace dropped. A new Boston Marathon record for the fastest time would not be set today.

*Enthusiastic fans watch the race from a balcony.*

*Mile after mile, the runners keep going.*

Toshihiko Seko, winner of the 1987 race, once made the comment that Boston Marathon friendships end at Boston College (the twenty-one-mile mark) and do not resume until the finish line. This, however, did not hold true for Hussein and Ikangaa, who were still leading the pack, running side by side. They did not separate until the turn from Hereford Street onto Boylston. With just over a quarter of a mile to go, Ikangaa had a slight lead. He cut the turn onto Boylston tight, forcing Hussein up and onto the curb. Hussein broke stride briefly. He then ran behind Ikangaa to draft him.

*Joan Benoit and Norway's Ingrid Kristiansen are both two-time winners of the Boston Marathon.*

With one hundred yards left, Hussein attempted to slingshot past Ikangaa. The rivals sprinted toward the finish line. After twenty-six miles, the race had come down to a 100-yard dash.

Hussein sprinted past Ikangaa to win the ninety-second Boston Marathon by one second. Their times, 2:08:43 and 2:08:44, became the marathon's second and third fastest. Their finish was the closest in Boston Marathon history.

And Hussein had finally put the African continent in the Boston record books.

Finishing the Boston Marathon takes stamina and determination.

## HEARTBREAK HILL

In 1990, Juma Ikangaa tried once again to win the Boston Marathon. After setting a record pace, Ikangaa hit the Newton hills —and discovered how Heartbreak Hill, the hill before Boston College, got its name. After running the hill, he became disoriented. Gelindo Bordin of Italy seized his opportunity. He passed Ikangaa and went on to win the marathon. Bordin became the first man in history to have won an Olympic Marathon and then a Boston Marathon.

Ikangaa went on to place second for the third year in a row. Visibly frustrated, he said he would be back again.

*The victorious Gelindo Bordin.*

## DATE DUE

| | | | |
|---|---|---|---|
| | | | |
| | | | |
| | | | |
| | | | |
| | | | |
| | | | |
| | | | |
| | | | |
| | | | |
| | | | |
| | | | |
| | | | |
| | | | |
| | | | |
| | | | |
| | | | |

FOLLETT